KT-558-456

C152055676

21st-century SCIENCE

TELECOMS

Present knowledge • Future trends

Written by Simon Maddison

W
FRANKLIN WATTS
LONDON•SYDNEY

First published in 2003 by

Franklin Watts
96 Leonard Street
London EC2A 4XD

Franklin Watts Australia
45-51 Huntley Street
Alexandria
NSW 2015

© Franklin Watts 2003

Design Billin Design Solutions
Editors Chris Oxlade, Sarah Ridley
Art Director Jonathan Hair
Editor-in-Chief John C. Miles
Picture Research Diana Morris

A CIP catalogue record for this book
is available from the British Library

ISBN 0 7496 4499 0

Printed in Hong Kong, China

Picture credits
Bettmann/Corbis: 14
Andrew Brookes/SPL: 4-5, 13
Mark Edwards/Still Pictures: front cover t
Humphrey Evans/Corbis: 34
Klein/Hubert/Corbis: 40
© ITU/A.de Ferron: 41, 45, 46-7, 48
LWA-Stephen Welstead/Corbis: 9
LWA-Dan Tardiff/Corbis: 25
Lawrence Manning/Corbis: 6-7, 23
André Maslennikov/Still Pictures: front
cover c, back cover, 1, 2-3, 28, 29
Minnesota Historical Society/Corbis: 36
© Net Gear: 24
© Nokia: front cover bc, 38
Leonard de Selva/Corbis: 8
© Trium: front cover bl & br, 39

*Whilst every attempt has been made to clear
copyright should there be an inadvertent
omission please apply in the first instance to the
publisher regarding rectification.*

KENT
ARTS & LIBRARIES
C152055676

Contents

the PACE of CHANGE

Before looking at the science and technology of telecommunications, let's define what telecommunications actually are. They are communications of information over a distance, using electricity, light and radio as the carriers.

Telecommunication devices let us speak to our friends, exchange messages instantly and watch live television pictures from the other side of the world. Today we take telecommunications for granted – so much for granted that it's worth imagining the world without them. Think about living in a world where messages could only move around at the speed of a sailing ship or a horse!

Over the last 150 years there have been huge changes in telecommunications, changes which are taking place at an ever-increasing rate.

Before telecommunications

Before the first telecommunication devices were invented, messages were carried by horse at an average speed of eight km/h (five mph). The introduction of railways in the nineteenth century increased this, but only to 20 km/h (12 mph).

1790–1860: The telegraph

The Chappe telegraph, developed in France in the 1790s, was a network of hilltop signalling stations, visible from one to the next. Each tower was hung with mechanical arms that were moved by pulleys to represent symbols and messages.

The electric telegraph was invented in the early 1800s, and went into commercial operation in the late 1830s. At first, the electric telegraph was only used locally, but by 1861 there was a coast-to-coast telegraph link across the United States of America.

1850: Telegraph cables

The first undersea telegraph cable was laid under the English Channel in 1850. Before this, messages were carried between England and France by boat. A transatlantic telegraph cable began working in 1866.

1890: Radio communication

The first radio communications took place in the 1890s, and Guglielmo Marconi sent the first transatlantic messages by radio in 1901. Radio allowed communication without wires, a huge advantage for ships. Its use in 1910 helped to capture the murderer, Dr. Crippen, when he was recognised on a ship. The captain radioed to shore and Crippen was arrested when the ship docked.

1962: Satellite transmission

The first telecommunications satellite, called Telstar, was launched in 1962. In 1963 millions of people around the world watched TV pictures, relayed by satellite, showing the assassination of US President John F. Kennedy, just minutes after it had happened.

1980s and 90s: Fax

A brief look at the story of the facsimile (fax for short) machine demonstrates the incredible pace of change in telecommunications today.

For most of the twentieth century, slow and expensive fax machines were used for special jobs, such as transmitting newspaper photographs. In the early 1980s new electronic technology allowed fast and cheap fax machines to be made. It seemed that the fax was here to stay. But in the space of about five years, in the 1990s, fax was largely overtaken by e-mail.

◄ ◄

Claude Chappe's telegraph, as shown in a French engraving of c.1800.

▼

The fax machine has largely been overtaken by e-mail.

the MESSAGE

The world of telecommunications is about sending (or 'transmitting') information or messages from one person to another, or from one machine to another. Telecommunications can be two-way (or interactive), as in the case of a telephone conversation, or one-way, as in the case of an e-mail or fax.

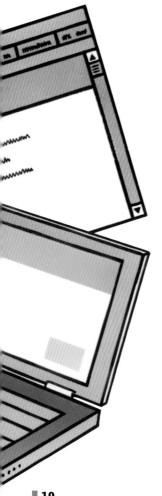

Telecommunications can also be broadcast, meaning that messages are sent from one person or machine to many people or machines at the same time.

Text

Text is made up simply of letters, numbers and other characters. Sending text is the oldest form of telecommunications. More than 100 years ago, text messages were sent via telegraph using codes such as Morse Code. Two forms of text communications are used frequently today. These are e-mails, sent via the Internet, and text messages, sent between mobile telephones using the short message service (SMS).

Audio

Voices, music and other sounds are forms of audio communication. The most common forms of audio are telephone conversations, radio conversations and radio broadcasting. Audio messaging, when you leave a 'voice mail' message on an answering machine, is also important. It is now increasingly popular to download MP3 music files over the Internet.

Images

Images are photographs, paintings, diagrams, writing and so on. Facsimile (fax) was the first method of sending images by telecommunications. It remains the simplest way of sending an image quickly from one place to another. Fax is still important for sending text in languages such as Japanese or Chinese, which use far more characters than alphabets in use in the West.

Increasingly, photographs are digital (see page 13), allowing images to be sent as attachments to e-mails. The combination of digital photography and mobile phones is likely to make sending messages with images extremely popular.

systems, are changing that. Video from webcams can also be watched live on the web, and video clips can be downloaded for watching later. In the future, video messages are likely to become as popular as voice and text messages.

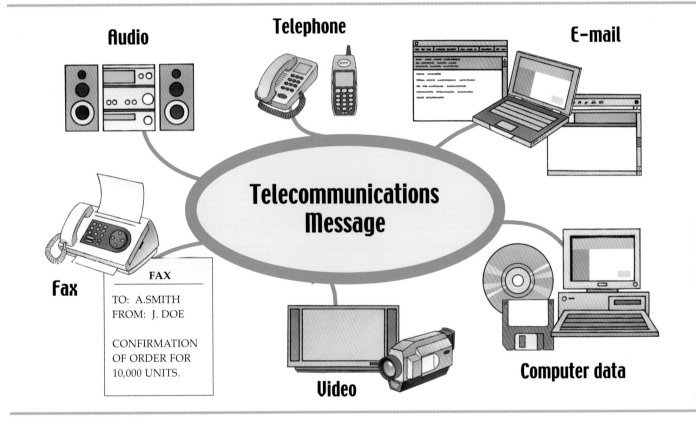

Video

Video is made up of moving images. It can be live or recorded. Television is the most common form of video communication. Normally you can only watch what the television stations broadcast, but interactive television and video-on-demand, both available via cable and satellite

Computer data

Data is exchanged by computers and other electronic machines. Examples of long-distance data communications are in banking and finance (such as between cash machines and central computers) and in the global-positioning system (GPS) for finding your way.

There can be many different ways of sending messages or information.

Signals, senders and receivers

To send (or 'transmit') information such as speech and photographs from one place to another using telecommunication systems, we need some way of representing it so that it can travel through the system.

Take speech, for example. Speech is made up of sound, and sound consists of waves of pressure that travel through the air. So to represent speech, we must represent the changes in air pressure caused by speech. This representation is called a signal.

Electrical signals for sound

The simplest telephone system is made up of two telephones, joined by a loop of copper wire that allows electricity to flow between them. One telephone is a transmitter. Its microphone detects the waves of air pressure made by its user speaking and turns them into an electrical signal. The signal travels round the wire loop to the other telephone, which is a receiver. Here, the signal makes the speaker earpiece vibrate to reproduce the original sound.

What is an electrical signal?

An electrical signal is simply an electric current, or flow of electricity. A current can only flow in a complete loop of wire called a circuit. In our simple telephone system, the transmitter makes the current change continuously in strength and direction. The changes represent the changing air pressure as someone speaks.

You can see an electrical signal represented visually using an oscilloscope. The oscilloscope displays the strength and direction of a current on its screen, making the signal look like a wave shape.

Analogue signals

When you compare the electrical signal from a telephone transmitter with the changes in air pressure it represents, the two match closely. Rises and falls in pressure are

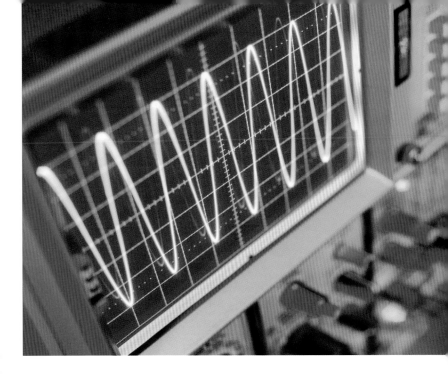

represented exactly by changes in current in the signal. The signal is said to be an 'analogue' or representation of the wave. The transmission of sound in this way is called analogue transmission.

All electrical signals naturally lose strength as they travel. This effect is called attenuation. They also get distorted and suffer from 'noise' or interference caused by other signals.

Digital signals

Since the 1970s there has been a rapid change from analogue transmission to digital transmission. A digital signal consists of a stream of on-off pulses (called a bit-stream) that represents a list of binary numbers. Some communication devices – such as computers – send information that is already in digital form. Analogue signals from other devices, such as telephones, are converted to digital form before they travel.

To do this, the strength of an analogue signal is measured, or 'sampled', at regular intervals Each sample is then turned into a number, linking to form a stream of numbers. At the other end, the signal is converted back into an analogue signal.

The advantages of digital

Digital transmission has huge advantages over analogue. Digital signals can also become weak and distorted but because digital signals are made up of pulses, the original signal can easily be recovered.

Another advantage of digital signals is that they can be used to represent any type of information. So sound, video and text are all represented by pulses, and can use the same equipment and routes.

All about waves

The height of a wave, called its amplitude, represents the strength of a signal. The distance between the crests is called the wavelength. The frequency of a signal is how often it changes direction every second.

▲

An oscilloscope shows an electrical signal as a wave.

▼

The component parts of a sound or electrical wave.

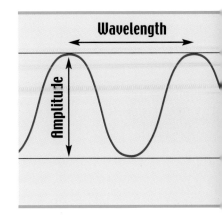

Wires, fibres and aerials

When you speak to a friend on the telephone, signals travel both ways between the two machines. Whether the signals are analogue or digital, they can travel in three different forms – as electricity, as light and as radio waves. They move by means of wires, optical fibres and through the air (or space) between radio aerials.

Wires and electricity

The simplest way to connect a transmitter and a receiver is by using an electric circuit of two wires. These wires are called a twisted pair, which means the wires are twisted together. This minimises interference from other signals. The telephone circuit from your house to the local telephone exchange probably uses copper wires. Telephone calls across the country and around the world may use large cables full of many thousands of copper wires.

Wire problems

Unfortunately attenuation – the gradual weakening of the signal as it travels along the wire – is a problem. Also the changing current that makes up a signal creates radio waves. These waves can affect the signal in wires nearby, causing 'crosstalk'. You may have experienced this when you have heard someone else's telephone conversation faintly in the background during a call. Despite these problems, a twisted pair is good enough to connect a telephone to the local telephone exchange several kilometres away. Co-axial cable (see page 22) reduces these problems, and is used over longer distances.

Signals that travel over large distances along wires are amplified regularly to restore their original strength. Co-axial submarine cables need amplifiers about every 10 km (six miles) all the way across the ocean – a big headache if anything goes wrong!

Optical fibres and light

An optical fibre is a very thin fibre of very pure glass that guides light from end to end. Signals travel along an optical fibre in digital form as pulses of light. At one end, the signal to be sent is converted from an electrical signal into pulses of light made by a tiny semiconductor laser. At the speed of light, the flashes reach the other end almost instantly, where they are converted back to an electrical signal.

Optical fibres have several advantages over wires. An incredible number of high-frequency signals can travel along the cable at the same time. With all signals, the higher the frequency of the signal, the more information can be fitted into the signal. So optical fibres have a very high capacity.

Another advantage is that there is very little attenuation in an optical fibre, and virtually no interference between fibres in the same cable.

Aerials and radio

Signals also travel in the form of radio waves. Radio waves are made at a transmitting aerial, travel through the air or space, and are picked up by a receiving aerial. A signal is transmitted by shaping a radio wave at the transmitter. This process is called modulation. Either the wave's amplitude is modulated (called AM) or its frequency is modulated (called FM). When the signal is received, it is recovered by demodulating the wave.

There is a whole range of radio waves, called the radio spectrum, with a wide range of frequencies. For telecommunications, the spectrum is divided into sections called bands. Different bands are used for different radio communications, such as mobile telephones, broadcast radio, walkie-talkie radio, and so on.

The obvious advantage of radio is that no cables are needed, hence the word 'wireless'.

◄◄
Alexander Graham Bell demonstrates his telephone in 1876. His invention relied on an electric circuit made up of wires – just the same as today.

Multiplexing

Telephone exchanges are linked to each other by co-axial cables, optical-fibre cables, terrestrial radio links and satellite links. These links must carry thousands of calls between the exchanges at the same time. It would be impossible to have a separate pair of wires, optical fibres or set of aerials to carry each individual call!

To allow links to carry thousands of calls, many signals are combined and sent along the same link. This process is called multiplexing. At the receiving end, the signals are separated, or de-multiplexed. There are several different ways of multiplexing.

Frequency-division multiplexing

Frequency-division multiplexing is used to send many analogue signals along the same radio link or wire. Several signals can be sent from one radio aerial to another by sending each one using a radio wave of a different frequency.

This works like a radio set where you find each radio station on a different frequency. In the same way, electrical signals of different frequencies can be used to carry signals. Each frequency carries a single phone call.

Digital multiplexing

Digital signals are multiplexed in a different way to analogue signals. Remember that a digital signal is a stream of binary numbers, transmitted in a stream of on-off pulses. To multiplex digital signals, a number from one signal is transmitted along a link, followed by a number from a second signal, and so on. After a number from each signal has been sent, the sequence is repeated. Each signal is allocated a time slot, and so this is known as time-division multiplexing.

With digital multiplexing, signals from different sources, such as telephones, video equipment and computers, can be mixed on a high-capacity digital link. Time-division multiplexing is the most common method of multiplexing on optical-fibre links. The capacity of optical fibres can be increased many times by using light of different colours. This is called wave-division multiplexing.

Code-division multiplexing

In code-division multiplexing, the spectrum of radio frequencies is not split up into narrow slots. Instead, signals are spread across the whole of the spectrum. Each signal is coded in a different way, and it is this unique code for each signal that is used to unscramble the signal at the receiver.

This works rather like the way you recognise voices. Imagine you are in a crowded room with lots of people talking. You can recognise someone you know from all the other voices, because of the specific characteristics of that voice, even though all the voices use the same sound waves.

Bandwidth

You will often hear the word 'bandwidth' in telecommunications.

Bandwidth originally meant a range of frequencies. For example, in frequency-division multiplexing, each signal takes up a particular range of radio frequencies, known as its bandwidth. The more complex the information a signal carries, the more bandwidth it requires. For example, the signal for a television picture contains thousands of times more information than the signal for a voice call. The television picture requires a bandwidth of about 6 megahertz; the voice call requires a bandwidth of about 2,400 kilohertz.

Bandwidth is also a measure of the capacity or speed of a digital telecommunications line. In this case, it is measured in the number of bits per second (bps) that can travel along it.

▼
Time-division multiplexing works rather like boxes being filled on a conveyor belt. Each 'box' is a time slot that is 'filled' with digital data.

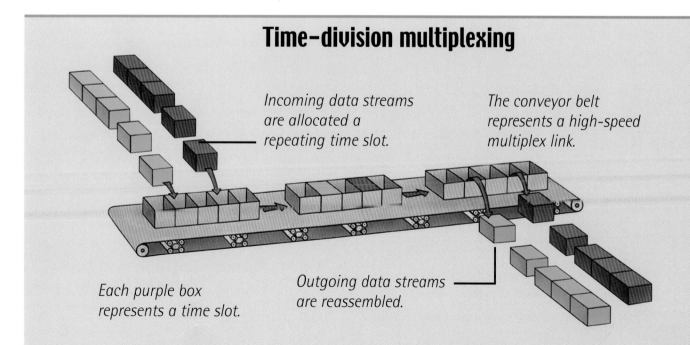

Time-division multiplexing

Incoming data streams are allocated a repeating time slot.

The conveyor belt represents a high-speed multiplex link.

Each purple box represents a time slot.

Outgoing data streams are reassembled.

NETWORKS

Transmitters and receivers, whether telephones, radio transmitters or computers, must be connected together by telecommunications links so that signals can travel between them. Together, the transmitters, receivers and links are called a network. There are three main types of network – circuit-switched networks, broadcast networks and packet-switched networks (see page 20).

Circuit-switched networks

Your telephone can be connected to any other telephone in the world, simply by dialling the right number. How is this achieved? By using switching stations called telephone exchanges where connections between telephones are set up.

Telephone exchanges were developed soon after Alexander Graham Bell invented the telephone in 1876. Originally these were manual systems, where an operator connected the wires together. They became automatic in the early 1900s.

At a telephone exchange, the electrical circuits from each telephone in an area come together. Local telephone exchanges are linked to each other through regional, national and international exchanges, allowing people in different areas and countries to call each other. When a person makes a call, the process of dialling sets up a connection, or circuit, between the two phones via all the telephone exchanges on the route. This sort of network is called a circuit-switched network.

The telephone network operates like a railway network, with local, regional and international routes and stations. In the same way that you catch a train and make connections, a telephone call is routed along local connections to get to the main (or 'trunk') network for travel between cities and countries.

Making networks efficient

In early telephone networks, when a person made a call, an individual electrical circuit was set up between the two telephones, using switches at each telephone exchange along the route. The part of the circuit connecting the telephone exchanges could not be shared while the call was taking place. Only when the call had finished could it be used to connect two other telephones.

During a conversation, it is usually only one person who talks at once, so both directions are rarely used at the same time. There are also lots of short pauses between words and phrases. All this means that a circuit is under-used. In the 1950s, complex systems were developed to get rid of the 'quiet bits' in phone calls, by switching bits of conversation quickly in and out of the system. These systems were complicated and expensive, but made it possible for international circuits to carry several phone calls at the same time. Today, these inefficiencies are increasingly being solved by the use of packet-switched networks (see page 20).

Broadcast networks

Radio and television networks are arranged very differently to telephone networks. There is one transmitter, and this sends out the same signal to all receivers. This is called broadcasting. Some radio stations, such as the one at Rugby in England, operate at very low frequencies, which allows their signals to be broadcast over the whole world. Broadcasting is also done over local-area networks and the Internet.

The telephone network is made up of a hierarchy of exchanges.

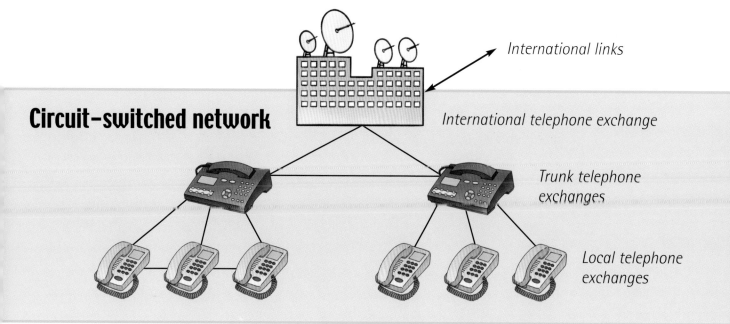

Circuit-switched network

International links

International telephone exchange

Trunk telephone exchanges

Local telephone exchanges

COMPUTER NETWORKS

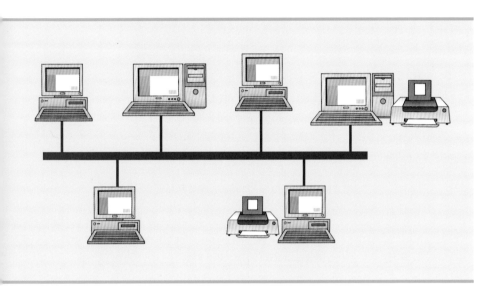

When you speak on the telephone, your voice creates a continuous stream of sound. This means that two telephones must be connected permanently together during a call so that the person at the other end can hear and understand you.

A local-area network (LAN) connects a group of computers and printers together.

Data from computers, however, comes in short, rather than continuous, bursts and so it can be handled in a different way from the sounds from a telephone. In a computer network, there are no exchanges and switches. The computers (and any printers, scanners, etc.) are connected together permanently by one complete circuit, which is shared. Unlike the telephone system, there is no need to set up a new circuit for each call. The connections are only used when they are needed. The network is idle when no data is being sent.

Packets of data

Before data is transmitted through a computer network, it is divided into chunks called packets, each of which can hold a small amount of data. A data packet is rather like a parcel that you post. It has an electronic 'wrapper' around it, containing the electronic address of the receiver. The packet of data is sent from the transmitter to the receiver, travelling around the network until it reaches the computer with the correct address. A network in which packets are moved around like this is called a packet-switched network.

Local, wide and global

In the computer network in a school, there may be a dozen computers and a printer connected together. This is known as a local-area network (LAN). Packets of data are sent around the network from one computer to another. Your local computer collects any passing packet with its address on.

A network that connects computers over a much larger area (perhaps all the computers of a company that has offices in different towns or countries) is called a wide-area network (WAN).

The Internet is a computer network that links millions of computers world-wide. It is a global-area network. It allows any computer to send data around the world.

Internet routers

The Internet is made up of thousands of machines called routers around the world, connected together by high-speed digital links. Packets of data are passed from router to router around the world. Like a super-high-speed mailman at the sorting office, the router looks at the address of every packet that comes to it, and sends it to another router, until it is finally delivered to the right computer.

Depending on how busy different links are and whether there are problems with any of the links, each packet may take a different route around the network. At the receiving end, the packets are collected and reassembled into the right order before being put back together again.

▼

Individual packets of data may take one of several different routes through a packet-switched network, such as the Internet.

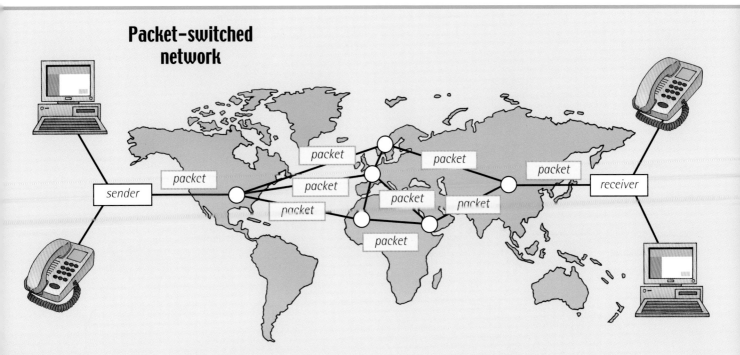

Packet-switched network

TERRESTRIAL communications links

Terrestrial communications links on the Earth's surface continue to carry the majority of telecommunications signals around the world. Terrestrial links are made up of electrical cables, optical–fibre cables and radio aerials. Imagine a call between a mobile telephone and a fixed–line telephone. The call is transmitted using radio waves, then by wires or optical–fibres, then by wires again.

Wires, fibres and aerials

Most homes and many businesses are connected to the local telephone exchange by twisted pair cables (a pair of thin copper wires, insulated and twisted together). The same cable carries signals for telephone calls, faxes, and, via a modem, computer data. The wires are either supported on telegraph poles above the ground or go through pipes under the pavement. The falling cost of optical fibres and the increasing use of the Internet mean that optical fibres are also being used.

Underground co-axial cables carry cable television signals. In a co-axial cable one conductor of the pair is surrounded by a tube formed by the other conductor. Insulating material separates the two elements. Cable companies use co-axial cable because it is less susceptible to interference and carries signals of a much higher frequency. Co-axial cables also form some 'trunk' connections between telephone exchanges up and down the country.

Long-distance links can be made by radio as well. In the telephone network, signals travel between dish-shaped aerials on hill tops and towers as microwaves.

Linking continents

International communications are carried in many ways. Many still travel along cables under the sea – submarine cables.

With the development of optical fibres, the capacity of submarine cables has increased many times. The first transatlantic submarine telephone cable in the 1950s could carry just 30 calls at the same time. TAT-9, an optical-fibre transatlantic cable laid in 1992, has a capacity of 80,000 calls.

New long-distance underground links are always provided by optical-fibre cables. The majority of the cost of laying a cable is taken up by digging a trench in the road and covering it up again, rather than with the cable itself. So it makes sense to lay cables with much more capacity than required. There is therefore much 'dark' optical fibre under the ground waiting to be used when demand rises.

Broadband connections

As the demand for the Internet increases, much of the communication network's bandwidth (or capacity) is being used up by data for e-mails, website access and downloading music and videos. In international communications links the amount of bandwidth used by data has now exceeded the amount used for telephone calls.

To cope with this demand, high-capacity or 'broadband' connections, such as ISDN and DSL, are being developed for homes and offices. These connections can carry hundreds of times more information than a standard telephone connection. ISDN, or Integrated Services Digital Network (see page 31), provides a bandwidth of 128 kbps to homes and offices along a twisted-pair cable. DSL (Digital Subscriber Line) provides data transmission rates up to 2 Mbps. It provides a broadband 'always on' type of connection.

▼
This photo of a handful of optical fibres demonstrates their light-transmitting ability.

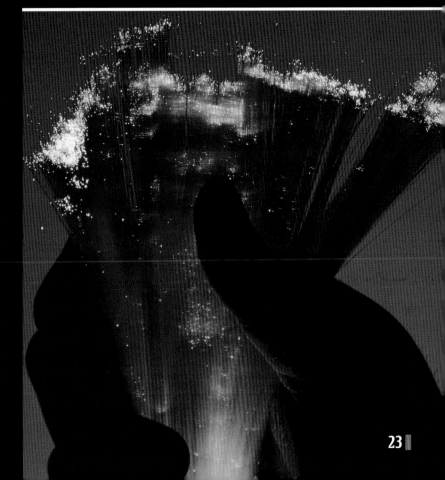

freedom from WIRES

Radio links are replacing wires as a way of linking communication devices, such as telephones and computers, to telecommunications networks. With a radio (or wireless) link, the devices can be moved about while still connected to the network, allowing mobile communications.

▲

A wireless local-area network (LAN) – a device that has the potential to revolutionise office communications.

During the 1990s, mobile communications in many countries changed from being a specialised, highly expensive service for professionals, to the most common form of speech communication. In fact, in countries with an underdeveloped telecommunications infrastructure, such as those in eastern Europe, it has been easier and quicker to develop a mobile communications network than to lay cables.

Short-range wireless

Short-range radio (over a few metres) is used to link computers into local-area networks. This is useful where laying wires would be difficult or time consuming, where temporary networks are needed (such as at exhibitions or events), and where users need to move around a lot in an office area or warehouse.

Several different systems (or 'standards') are competing in the wireless local-area network (LAN) market. One standard you might have heard of is called Bluetooth. It is used for communicating between mobile telephones and personal computers, as well as between mobile telephones and their ear pieces (which means no more wires).

Infrared

Infrared is used for short-range communication between personal computers, personal digital assistants (PDAs) and mobile telephones. This technology evolved from the humble television remote control. The drawback with infrared is that there must be a line of sight between the devices for the signals to travel between them.

Where next with wireless?

So where is the wireless revolution going? For many people, such as sales people permanently on the move, a mobile telephone is more useful than a fixed-line telephone. Mobile telephones will not completely displace fixed-line phones, but they are likely to become more common. The mobile telephone will develop into a complete personal communicator. It will be able to connect automatically into any communications system.

In a similar way, radio-equipped computers will become common. They will also connect up to the local communications system. For example, a notebook computer switched on in an airport or coffee shop will automatically connect to the Internet and to a local printer. In an office, the same computer will connect up to the office network. All devices, from mobile telephones to computers, will be able to communicate with each other.

Wireless devices will provide more and more functions. They will include cameras, music players, video players, and so on. Some of these goods are just beginning to appear on the market.

Some telecommunications companies provide global mobile services utilising communications satellites. However, this now looks as though it will be limited to use on ships and in remote areas where standard mobile telephones are out of the range of their networks.

▼

Wireless devices permit laptops to connect to local communications systems and the Internet.

Cellular MOBILE systems

The recent revolution in mobile telephones has been brought about by the development of cellular mobile communications networks. From small beginnings in the 1980s, these had become the most important means of telephone communication by the end of the 1990s. Why are they so successful?

Cells vary in size depending on how many mobiles are expected to be in use within a cell at any one time. The transmitter and receiver within each cell have a limited capacity.

Firstly, compared to fixed-line networks, cellular networks are cheap and quick to install. Secondly, developments in digital electronic technology, in radio aerial design, and in batteries, have all allowed manufacturers to make small, cheap, reliable and convenient mobile telephones.

Cellular operation

The two main problems for the designers of mobile telephone systems are the limited amount of transmitting power available in a small mobile telephone, and the limited amount of the overall radio spectrum that is available for mobile communications.

To overcome these problems, geographical areas are divided into chunks called cells – hence the term cellular telephones. In each cell there is a transmitter and receiver that receives signals from, and sends signals to, any telephone in the area. Cells next to each other operate on different radio frequencies to avoid interference, but cells some distance apart can use the same frequency as each other. This cellular arrangement means that cellular telephones can operate over short-range radio links, reducing the power needed, and also that the same frequencies can be re-used in different parts of the country.

The transmitter and receiver in each cell have a limited capacity, so only a restricted number of people can use their telephones in the same cell. This is obviously a problem in busy places such as cities and airports. So to increase the call capacity in these locations, cells are made smaller and the number of cells is increased. There are now 'micro-cells' covering a range of a just a few hundred metres, and even 'pico-cells', which serve just a small part of an office building.

Cellular standards

Modern cellular systems are called second generation (or 2G) networks. They all use digital radio transmissions that allow clear, high-quality sound transmission.

The Global System for Mobiles (GSM) system is used across Europe and widely around the rest of the world. It uses three different radio bands in different countries, but dual and tri-band mobile telephones are available that allow one telephone to work wherever it is in the world. GSM uses a time-division multiplex system.

Japan has led the world with a technology called i-mode, which allows mobile phone users to access information services in a similar way to the Internet. Similar data services are supported by the General Packet Radio System (GPRS) service, which is an extension of GSM. This is sometimes called 2.5G.

More speed and performance is promised by the third generation (3G) standard. This is expected to become widely available in the next few years. Second generation cellular systems can provide perhaps up to 14 kbps data rates, 2.5G provides 28 to 40 kbps, and 3G promises up to 2 Mbps – good enough for live video to be sent to a telephone.

▼

High-capacity links with normal telephone networks allow two-way connections between land lines (terrestrial telephones) and mobiles.

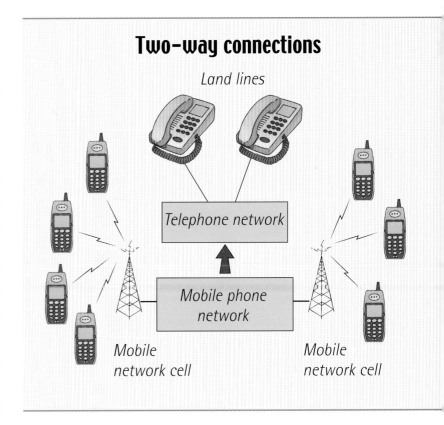

Two-way connections

Land lines

Telephone network

Mobile phone network

Mobile network cell

Mobile network cell

SATELLITE
communications

Before the first telecommunications satellite was launched in the 1960s, long-distance communications could only be carried by submarine cables and long-distance radio links. Submarine cables are still used on major routes, but are not economic for smaller countries and islands. These only need a small dish aerial for satellite communications. Long-distance radio links are affected too much by atmospheric conditions to be reliable.

A telecommunications satellite works as a relay station in space. Radio signals in the form of microwaves are sent up to a satellite from a dish-shaped aerial at a ground station, aimed at the satellite. The satellite collects the signal, boosts it, and transmits it back down, again as microwaves, to a dish-shaped aerial at the receiving ground station. A satellite can be shared by many ground stations.

Geostationary satellites

Most communications satellites sit in an orbit about 36,000 km (22,500 miles) above the Earth's equator. At this altitude, they orbit the Earth at the same rate as the Earth spins on its axis, and so they stay above the same area on the surface all the time.

Geostationary satellites have two main advantages. The first is that one satellite can 'see' about a third of the Earth's surface, and so can provide point-to-point communication anywhere in this area. The second advantage is that, because a geostationary satellite stays in the same place above the Earth's surface, it is easy to aim signals at it. The disadvantage is that, even at the speed of light, a signal takes approximately a quarter of a second to get up to a geostationary satellite and down again. This delay is noticeable in a phone conversation, and is long enough to make a elephone call via two satellites very difficult. You sometimes notice the same delay on the television news, when a correspondent is reporting from the other side of the world.

Low–Earth orbit satellites

Low-Earth orbit satellites sit in much lower orbits than geostationary satellites, between about 200–1,000 km (120–620 miles) above the surface of the Earth. Signals that travel via them do not suffer significant delays. The satellites are also suitable for direct communication with low-power devices such as hand-held telephones. However, they do have their disadvantages. A low-Earth orbit satellite can cover only a small area of the surface, and many of them are needed for global coverage. They also move quickly across the sky, so are more difficult for ground stations to keep track of. Another disadvantage is that, they have a shorter lifetime than stationary satellites as they are very gradually slowed down by the thin atmosphere, and eventually fall out of orbit.

Satellite operators

For many years Inmarsat has provided communications services to ships at sea, and coverage is now extended to people in remote locations on land.

In the 1990s there was a major move by companies such as Iridium and Globalstar to provide global mobile telephone services using satellites. So far these have been commercially unsuccessful. The handsets are large and unwieldy and because of the huge costs of launching the satellites, operating costs and call charges are extremely high. They have also been overtaken by the convenience and economy of cellular telephones.

▼

Large dishes transmit and receive information from orbiting communications satellites.

the INTERNET

The Internet is a computer network that reaches right around the world, and so is a global-area network. It has rapidly become the global-area network that most people use for almost all types of personal and business communications, except telephone calls.

Network connections

The Internet is a packet-switched network (see page 20) of interconnected computers. These computers are either personal computers in homes and offices or powerful machines called servers that store web pages and e-mails.

The links in the Internet are routers, – high-speed digital devices – which are connected together by high-capacity data communication circuits. Routers must handle enormous numbers of packets extremely quickly to prevent the network from overloading. The Internet is being constantly extended and expanded to provide additional data transmission capacity and to allow more users to connect at the same time.

Packet delays

Computers and routers often have to wait their turn to send packets of data. In cases like this packets are held in a special store called a buffer until there is a gap in the traffic. The delays caused by data packets being stored in buffers at the routers are often frustrating when you are downloading complex web pages.

These delays are a big problem for certain types of data, such as continuous (or 'streaming') music and video. Over the web video can be slow, jerky and interrupted and often the sound and picture will arrive at different times. Much research is in progress to overcome this problem, and allow good quality live voice and video to travel the Internet.

Dial-up Internet access

Most homes are connected to the Internet via a dial-up connection. This means they connect temporarily by an ordinary telephone line using a modem. The modem turns the digital computer data into an analogue signal that can travel down the line.

ISDN

ISDN (Integrated Services Digital Network) is a system that allows an ordinary, twisted pair phone line to carry digital signals to and from a computer, as well as digital telephone calls. ISDN brings the advantages of digital transmission to people's homes, and provides a direct digital link to the Internet. It needs a special box that is an analogue-to-digital converter and multiplexor all in one. ISDN is also a dial-up connection, but it can handle much greater amounts of data than a modem.

DSL

DSL (Digital Subscriber Line) uses similar technology to ISDN, but allows a permanent, rather than a dial-up, connection. DSL permits data access and telephone calls to take place at the same time. DSL comes in several forms, such as ADSL (Asymmetric Digital Subscriber Line), which takes account of the fact that you will normally want to receive much more data than you send. Another form is HDSL, which simply stands for High-speed Digital Subscriber Line.

This diagram shows different types of connections to the Internet's 'information superhighway'.

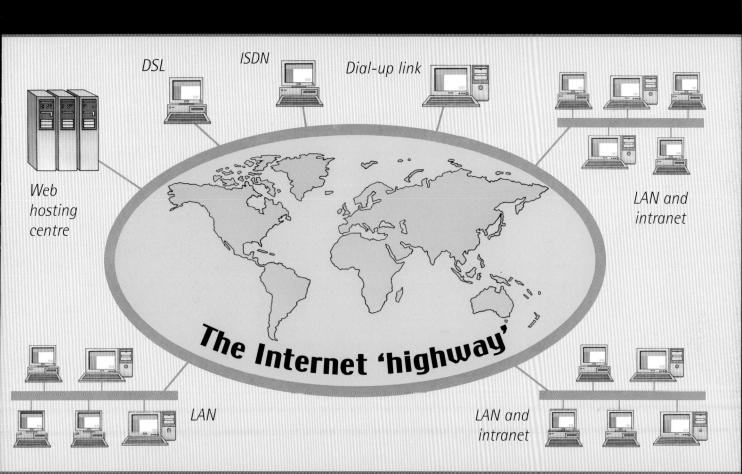

DSL   ISDN   Dial-up link

Web hosting centre

LAN and intranet

The Internet 'highway'

LAN

LAN and intranet

INTERNET CONTROL

Two major features of the Internet control how data packets travel around the network and reach the correct computer. They are communication protocols and packet addressing.

Communication protocols

A protocol is a set of rules used by computers to exchange data. A protocol might allow the data sent by one computer to be understood by another, or allow computers to tell each other when to send data and when it has been received. The Internet uses two protocols – Internet Protocol (IP), which controls how data packets are made up and addressed, and TCP (Transmission Control Protocol), which controls the movement of the packets. Together they are known as TCP/IP.

Packets can be delayed and mixed up in transmission, so that they do not arrive in the order that they were sent. They can also get lost completely because of 'collisions' in the network, overflowing buffers and interference. TCP handles these problems. It makes sure that received packets are put back into the right sequence, acknowledges the receipt of packets, and requests the re-transmission of lost or corrupted packets.

Internet addressing

You can think of a packet moving through the Internet in the same way as a letter moving through the postal system. Each packet has an Internet address included in it, just as every letter has an address written on it. When a letter reaches a sorting office, it is put in a box that will go to the main sorting office of the region that it is addressed to, and sent on. At the next sorting office, it is sent on again. This continues until the local sorting office delivers it to its destination address.

On the Internet, routers work like postal sorting offices. They read the address on a packet and send it onto the next correct router, until the packet reaches its destination computer.

A local-area network has a router that connects to the Internet. The router knows which addresses are local, and can be delivered on the local-area network, and which are not. All packets with non-local addresses are sent out over the Internet to the router at an Internet service provider (ISP). This router is more powerful, and has more complex routing information. It processes the packets and sends them on their way.

Addressing hierarchy

All Internet addresses (or IP addresses) have four parts. Each part is a number between 0 and 255. The parts are separated by full stops. Generally an address is written in the form AAA.BBB. CCC.DDD. The address is a bit like a postal address, where you could think of the DDD part as the number of your house on the street, the CCC part as the name of your street, BBB as the name of your town or region, and the AAA as your country.

This form of addressing gives a total of 255 x 255 x 255 x 255 different possible addresses – that's more than four billion. However, in the future this may not be enough, and a new addressing system is slowly being introduced which will allow for many more addresses.

Computers on local-area networks will have addresses that are different only in the DDD part. These are called class D addresses. If necessary a packet will be sent all the way to a class A router to determine the correct destination.

▼
This picture shows the similarities between an Internet address and an ordinary postal address.

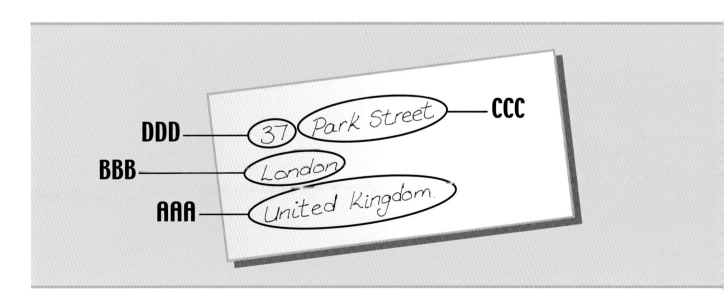

BROADCASTING

Broadcasting networks transmit radio and television programmes. In a broadcast system, transmitters send signals to many receivers at the same time, using radio aerials, cables and satellites.

Radio

Radio broadcast signals are either transmitted by amplitude modulation (AM) or frequency modulation (FM).

In amplitude modulation the original analogue signal is used to vary (or modulate) the amplitude (or wave height) of a radio signal. AM broadcasting is simple to set up and the receivers are cheap to manufacture. Its disadvantage is that the signal is very susceptible to interference, noise and distortion.

You will have noticed this if you have listened to AM radio stations at night or in a car. At night the characteristics of the Earth's atmosphere change, and it reflects radio waves back down to Earth much more easily. This allows signals from far away to be heard, but also means there is more interference between different radio stations.

In frequency modulation (FM) the frequency of the radio signal is modulated by the analogue signal. This makes the signal far less susceptible to distortion and noise, and allows for much higher quality reception. However, FM reception tends to be either good or bad. When the signal gets too weak, reception disappears rather than getting fainter.

Television signals

A television image is made up of many thin horizontal lines. In the UK system – called PAL – there are 625 lines. The USA uses a system called NTSC, with 525 lines. And in France the SECAM system, like the UK, also uses 625 lines.

In all these systems, a fresh image has to be transmitted more than 50 times a second in order to create the impression of a moving picture. The signal for a picture has to include all the information about the colour and brightness along each line, where the line is on the screen, where it starts and finishes, and where the next picture starts.

Colour television signals are broken into three parts for each line, one for each primary colour (red, green and blue). This means that the process of modulation is much more complex than for radio. Television signals are susceptible to noise and distortion. One typical problem is 'ghosting', where a second faint picture appears next to the first.

Transmission and coverage

In terrestrial broadcasting by radio waves, both radio and television signals are transmitted from aerials placed in high locations, such as on hilltops and at the top of tall masts. This gives wide coverage because the signals can be detected over a large area. Television usually uses higher frequency waves than radio, partly because a television signal requires a far higher bandwidth.

Satellite television

Satellite is now a very common means of broadcasting television programmes. The altitude of a satellite means that it has much wider coverage than a conventional television transmitter. Satellite transmission has opened up television to an international market because programmes can be picked up in many different countries.

Digital broadcasting

Digital technology has made its way into radio and television, and digital radio and television will become the norm within five to ten years. Digital broadcasting uses the same techniques of sampling and coding as telephone signals, although extremely high sampling rates and very high bandwidths are needed for television pictures. The use of digital means that additional data can be carried with a picture, such as subtitles in a different language.

◄ ◄

Most television signals are still broadcast from tall masts, such as this one.

THE big ISSUES

Since it began, the telecommunications industry has constantly faced challenges. The main challenge has been to satisfy the ever-growing demand for telecommunications, along with the desire for quicker, more reliable and secure communications.

The demand for telecommunications is created by the increasing number of users, the greater range of services they want, the increased amount of time spent communicating, and the larger amount of data being transmitted.

The need for bandwidth

The limited bandwidth of fixed telephone lines to homes and offices is a barrier to such things as fast Internet access and high-quality video telephones. Greater bandwidth allows fast downloading of complex web pages.

The fixed-line telephone network was built for the small bandwidth required for voice calls. It has struggled to keep pace with the rapid development of the Internet. Technologies such as ISDN and DSL (see page 31) have extended the capacity of the humble twisted-pair telephone line beyond the imagination of engineers working 20 years ago. But even DSL is unlikely to satisfy demand for long!

Optical fibre has the potential for staggering increases in bandwidth, but laying optical-fibre cables to every home will be a long and expensive operation.

The radio spectrum

The radio spectrum is the range of radio waves of different frequencies used for telecommunications. However, the radio spectrum is a finite resource. There is only so much of it to go around.

Until the 1990s, the radio spectrum was used mainly by broadcasters. The rise of mobile radio communications, such as mobile telephones, has changed that, and squeezing more slots into the radio spectrum is a huge challenge.

Decreasing the size of cells, and increasing the number of radio base stations is likely to be the answer to this problem. However this raises both environmental issues (because of the number of base stations needed), financial issues (because of the costs involved), and health issues (because of concerns about radio waves from mobile telephones harming our health).

Addressing systems

The earliest telephone switching systems were manual. Addressing was easy – in those days when you lifted your receiver you were connected to a human operator, who manually connected your line to the line of the person you wanted to speak to. In 1910, in the Chinatown district of San Francisco, USA, a 10,000-line manual exchange operated using only the names of the users!

This system became impractical as more and more people bought telephones, and so telephone numbers (and automatic exchanges that allowed direct dialling) were introduced. A telephone number is the 'address' of a telephone, rather than of a person. In the same way, an Internet address (see page 33) is the address of a computer, not a computer user.

Mobile telephones tend to be associated with a person rather than a location (such as a house or office), as fixed-line telephones are. It may be possible to revert back to the pioneering days of telephony, where your telephone 'address' once again becomes your name, allowing people to call you by name rather than by number. It would work in a similar way to e-mail addresses.

◄ ◄

The capacity of an early telephone exchange was limited because calls were manually connected with wires and jacks.

the FUTURE

A number of trends in the world of telecommunications became clear in the last decade of the twentieth century. Here is a summary of those trends, and how they will affect telecommunications in the next decade. Whether people will use them is much more difficult to predict!

▲

With the ability to send full-colour pictures, mobile phones now offer more than just sound and text messaging.

Multi-function devices

At the moment most communication devices have only one function. There are hand-held personal organisers, mobile telephones, MP3 players, CD players, radios, digital cameras, game devices, and so on. This means you need separate devices for each task – to play computer games, to make telephone calls and to listen to music.

Multi-function devices can perform two or more functions. Personal computers have been multi-function devices for some time. They can store and play music, videos and photographs; they can also be used to create or edit all three. As processing power increases and memory becomes smaller and cheaper, the same flexibility is beginning to appear in hand-held devices. Hand-held personal digital assistants with mobile phone functions built in are on the market, as are mobile phones with integral MP3 storage and playback. We are now seeing the first mobile telephones with an integral digital camera, allowing you to send snapshots instantly to your friends.

As prices fall and power and complexity increase, it will become increasingly easy to incorporate several functions into a single, powerful hand-held package, and, importantly, at a price that most people can afford. We are at a very early stage in this process of 'integration'.

Mobile and wireless

The rapid spread and popularity of mobile telephones has shown that 'mobile' will be the way forward. In the not-too-distant future all devices will incorporate some form of mobile operation. For example, you will be able to download music directly to an MP3 player, rather than via a personal computer, and you will be able to send digital photographs directly from your digital camera to other people.

Multi-function devices will be able to work together by communicating with each other via short-range radio links. Some mobile devices are already so small that it is difficult to enter information via a keypad. Voice recognition, now still in its infancy, will solve this problem.

Permanent connections

The concept of a telephone 'call' will disappear as both mobile and fixed-line devices become connected to the network all the time. The Internet will become the network that carries all types of communications.

Each user will have his or her own unique address, and he or she will have it for life. A communication device will keep track of a person's position and environment (such as home or office). It will then decide, for example, whether to take a message from a business client, if the person is at home, or let it ring through.

▼

Some of the latest planned wireless communication devices look like a cross between a telephone and jewellery. These are by Trium.

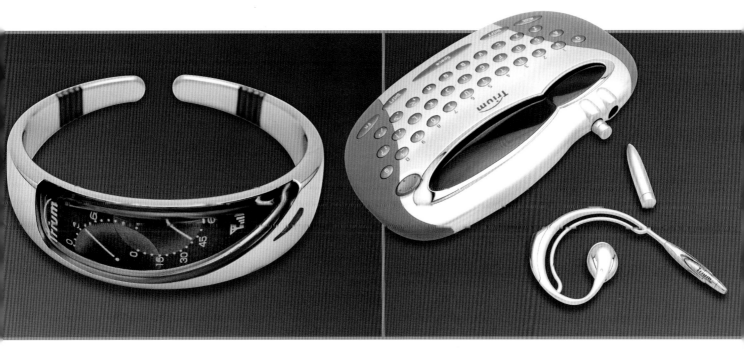

THE IMPACT OF TELECOMMUNICATIONS

Far more than any other factor, the advances in telecommunications have changed the pace of life and made the world feel like a smaller place.

News, politics and business

Telecommunications allow news from almost any part of the world to reach the rest of the world in an instant. This has a huge impact on our ideas about the world, and on public opinion. Information about events can no longer be controlled by governments, as it was in the past. News comes through too many channels, including the Internet, to allow this to happen today.

This has had an enormous impact on international affairs and attitudes. The reality of what is happening in far-off parts of the world is impossible to ignore – images of war, suffering and deprivation are sent into our living rooms every day.

Telecommunications enable businesses to operate conveniently right around the world, to trade with each other, to collaborate with each other, and to design and manufacture products in widely spread locations. World financial markets, in the USA, Europe and the Far East, can be integrated and can operate on a rolling basis as daylight moves around the world.

Telecommunications (especially the telephone and e-mail) also allow friends and relations scattered around the globe to keep in contact easily. The Internet allows international groups of people with common interests to discuss their interests and develop new and exciting ideas.

The global village

Telecommunications can help bring the world ever closer together, creating the idea of 'the global village'. So informed, this global community is aware of the problems, views, sufferings and achievements of others in the world. It is a community that can share new challenges, ideas and visions. By working together more closely, the people of the global community can create a better world for us all to live in.

A final thought

The International Telecommunications Union holds a world exhibition once every four years. In 1998 it was opened by Nelson Mandela, then president of the Republic of South Africa. He observed that half the people in the world had never even made a telephone call. For the rest of us, who would feel lost without our mobile phones, computers and Internet access, the real challenge of the twenty-first century must surely be to broaden access to telecommunications to everyone on the planet.

◄ ◄

Solar powered telephones, such as this example in Australia, now allow remote areas to be connected to the telephone network.

▼

Nelson Mandela speaks at the International Telecommunications Union exhibition in 1998.

GLOSSARY

amplify, amplification
Boosting the strength of an electrical or radio wave by increasing its amplitude.

amplitude
The amplitude of a wave is the height of its peaks.

analogue
An analogue signal is the image of a completely different signal, such as the sound waves in air.

attenuation
The loss in strength of a signal as it travels over a long distance.

band
A small slice of the radio spectrum.

bandwidth
A range of frequencies from the radio spectrum. The more complex a signal is, the more bandwidth it requires.

broadband
A high-speed connection that allows large amounts of data to be sent and received very quickly.

cell
The area covered by a mobile phone network transmitter.

circuit
A circuit is a conducting loop, typically of copper wire, that allows electric current to flow.

co-axial cable
A cable where one conductor is a tube and the other is carried in the middle of the tube.

de-multiplex
The process of separating out all the combined signals from a multiplexed link.

digital transmission
The way in which an analogue signal is coded and transmitted as a series of pulses.

electric current
The flow of electrical energy.

frequency
The frequency of a wave is the number of peaks that flow past a point in one second.

global-area network
A global-area network connects computers and LANs together around the world.

infrared
Light waves that are too low in frequency to see. Used for controlling your TV from a distance.

Internet
A global data network accessible by computers all around the world.

intranet
A private Internet, typically within a company or university.

LAN (local-area network)

A network that connects computers and printers together in a small area, such as an office.

modem

A modem converts data into electrical signals that can be transmitted over a telephone line.

modulation

The way in which an electrical or radio wave is altered in order to carry a signal. A modem modulates a wave at the sending end and de-modulates it at the receiving end; hence the name modulator-demodulator or 'modem' for short.

MP3 file

A popular way of storing a piece of music as digital data.

multiplex

The combining of many different signals to carry them over a single link.

optical fibre

A very thin fibre of pure glass, which can carry light for very long distances. Glass fibre can bend around corners.

oscilloscope

An instrument which visually displays electrical signals.

radio

Radio waves are similar to light waves, but operate at much lower frequencies. Like light, radio waves can travel long distances.

radio spectrum

The full range of radio waves from very low to extremely high frequencies.

sampling

The regular measurement of an analogue signal to enable it to be converted into a digital form.

telephone exchange

A switch that connects your telephone to someone else's, according to the numbers that you dial.

transmission

A transmission is the signal or group of signals that is sent from one location to another.

trunk network

A trunk network carries a large number of telephone calls between cities and countries.

twisted pair

Two electrical wires that are twisted together to minimise interference.

wavelength

The wavelength of a wave is the distance between its peaks. The longer the wavelength, the lower the frequency.

WAN (wide-area network)

A wide-area network connects computers and LAN's together over wide distances, such as between offices in different cities and countries.

21st-century SCIENCE

INDEX

A

aerials, radio 14-15, 16, 22, 26, 28, 29, 34, 35
amplitude 13, 15, 42
attenuation 13, 14, 15, 42

B

bands, radio 15, 27
bandwidth 17, 23, 35, 36-37, 42
Bell, Alexander Graham 14, 15, 18
bit-stream 13
broadband 23, 42
buffer 30, 32

C

cable, co-axial 15, 16, 22, 42
optical-fibre 14, 15, 16, 22, 23, 24, 37, 43
submarine 9, 15, 23, 28
transatlantic 9, 23
circuit, electric 12, 14, 15, 18, 19, 42
computer 11, 13, 16, 18, 20, 21, 22, 24, 25, 30, 32, 33, 37, 38, 39, 41, 42, 43

D

data 11, 17, 20, 21, 22, 23, 27, 30, 31, 32, 35, 36, 42, 43
digital 13, 16, 43
packet 20, 21, 30, 32, 33
DSL 23, 31, 36

E

e-mail 9, 10, 11, 23, 30, 37, 41
electricity 8, 12

F

facsimile machine (fax) 9, 10, 11
fax (message) 10, 22
fibres, optical see cable, optical-fibre

G

Global System for Mobiles (GSM) 27
General Packet Radio System (GPRS) 27

I

Inmarsat 29
ISDN 23, 31, 36
Internet 10, 19, 21, 22, 23, 25, 27, 30-31, 32-33, 36, 37, 39, 40, 41, 42
addressing 32-33
intranet 31, 42

L

light, infrared 24, 25, 42
links, telecoms 16-17, 18, 22-23, 24

M

Marconi, Guglielmo 9
microwaves 28
modulation 15, 34-35, 43

N

modem 22, 30, 31, 43
MP3 10, 38, 39, 43
multiplexing 16-17, 27, 42, 43

N

network 18-19, 24
broadcast 18-19, 34-35
cellular 26-27
circuit-switched 18-19
computer 20-21, 24, 25, 30, 42
global-area 21, 30, 42
local-area 20-21, 24, 31, 33, 42, 43
packet-switched 18-21, 30
wide-area (WAN) 21, 43

O

oscilloscope 12, 13, 43

P

photographs 9, 10, 11, 12
digital 11, 32, 38, 39

R

radio 8, 9, 10, 14-15, 16, 17, 18, 19, 22, 24, 28, 34, 35, 38

S

satellite 9, 11, 16, 25, 28-29, 34, 35

signals, analogue 12-13, 14, 16, 30, 34, 42, 43
digital 13, 14, 15, 16, 31, 42, 43
electrical 12, 13, 14, 15, 16, 42, 43
multiplexing 16-17
spectrum, radio 15, 17, 26, 37, 42, 43

T

telegraph 9, 10
Chappe 8, 9
telecommunications
audio 10, 11
demand for 36-37
satellite 28-29
telephone 10, 11,12, 13, 14, 15, 16, 18, 19, 20, 22, 23, 24, 25, 26, 28, 30, 31, 36, 38, 41
exchange 14, 18, 36, 43
mobile 10, 11, 15, 22, 24, 25, 26-27, 29, 37, 38, 39, 42
television 8, 9, 11, 17, 19, 22, 24, 25, 29, 34, 35, 42

V

video 11, 13, 16, 23, 25, 27, 30

W

wave, radio 14, 15, 16, 22, 28, 34, 37, 42, 43
web 11, 23, 30, 36
wires 14, 15, 16, 22, 24-25